Blue Dolphin Adventures

Copyright

Ⓒ

Bucur Loredan 10-02-2025
Birmingham U.K.

Contents:

Chapter 1: Meeting with the unknown

Chapter 2: Preparations for travel

Chapter 3: The first obstacle

Chapter 4: Unexpected friendship

Chapter 5: In the footsteps of legends

Chapter 6: Meeting with shark

Chapter 7: Dark caves

Chapter 8: Test of courage

Chapter 9: Unexpected help

Chapter 10: Hurricane

Chapter 11: The secret island

Chapter 12: The ancient secrets

Chapter 13: The road to Abis

Chapter 14: The monster in the depths

Chapter 15: Facing the pearls thieves

Chapter 16. Blue and the pearl of time

Chapter 17: The teaching of the elderly

Chapter 18: Return home

Chapter 19: Salvation plan

Chapter 20: Final confrontation

Chapter 21: The reef is reborn

Chapter 22: A new adventure

Chapter 23: Final attempts

Chapter 24: Sacrifice

Chapter 25: Meeting

Chapter 26: Lessons learned

Chapter 27: A new beginning

Chapter 28: Blue's legend

Chapter 1: Meeting with the unknown

The morning sun penetrated through the clear waters of the reef,throwing golden rays over the corals of all shapes and colors.Tropicals danced among the stone cracks,while the gentle waves swayed the marine vegetation.In the middle of this vibrant world lived Blue,a young dolphin with eyes.Big and full of curiosity.He had gathered around a wise old man,Nimbus,who was smoothing his dorsal swimming with a mysterious air.He knew that Nimbus had been everywhere,beyond the safe limits of the reef,and that he hid secrets that only the bravest could discover.He approached curiously,trying to listen.
-It is said,the deep voice began,that beyond this reef,where the water becomes dark and the currents are strong,there is a mysterious world.A place where the sunlight penetrates hard,where strange creatures are hidden in the shadows.That there are submerged cities,others talk about lost treasures and missing ships.But no one from here dared to go there and return to tell us what he saw.An unknown world? Hidden treasures? Mysterious creatures? It sounds exactly like the adventure he had always sought.He turned to his best,coral friend,a slightly more cautious,but loyal dolphin.
-What do you say,Coral? Don't you want to see with your eyes what's beyond the reef? Blue asked with a wide smile.Coral ripped off his caution.
-I don't know,Blue.If no one returned from there,maybe it's a good reason not to venture.But Blue could not be so easy.Gaining at the unknown aroused his imagination,and the desire to discover new things was Stronger than fear.So,in the evening,after the reef was quiet and the other dolphins were preparing for rest,Blue slowly headed for the edge of the reef.Where the crystalline blue became a dark blue,was the

unknown. They stirred deep and took the first step outside the world he knew. Immediately change, the currents were louder, the sounds more stifled, and the bottom of the ocean seemed to descend into a abyss. Without end. Everything, something was drawn before. It was a strange feeling, as if the ocean itself was called. As it was, he observed how the marine creatures were changing. Huge jellyfish floated ghostly, and the marine plants became rarer and more twisted, like arms trying to catch it. All of them, Blue continued their way, enchanted by the strange beauty of the place. Suddenly, you feel a change in a water. A cold current pushed him back slightly, and in the distance, something seemed to move in the dark. Blue held his breath. A huge silhouette was floating above him, almost invisible in the darkness of deep waters. Then, from a corner of the gaze, He saw a pair of bright eyes fixing him. The heart was beating. Something was there, hidden in the dark. He did not know whether to run or stay. But before he could make a decision, the mysterious silhouette was moving. He moved slowly, as if he studied it. Blue gathers his courage.

-Who are you? he asked in a shy voice. From the shadow, there was a

deep sound,almost like a lost echo.
-Who are you,little? It was a gentle voice,but full of power.Blue proudly directed his swimmer.
-It are Blue.And I am looking for the unknown.The silue is slightly,and the moon that pierced the water revealed the outlines of a huge whale,with the skin marked by deep wrinkles,signs of a long and full life.
-A curious dolphin,said the whale with a light smile.
-I still see such brave spirits.But you take care,Blue,because the unknown is not always friendly.Blue felt a mixture of fear and enthusiasm.

Chapter 2: Preparations for travel

Blue woke up early,illuminated by the gentle rays of the sun that penetrated through the crystalline waves of the reef.The man had not been restful,his thoughts about his journey filling his mind with enthusiasm and anxiety.When he heard the legend about the mysterious world beyond the reef,no he could also think of something else.He understood that he had to discover that world with his eyes.But for this,he needed serious preparations.Unknown advances needed caution,and Blue knew he could not leave without being prepared.
-He made courage and went to say goodbye to his family.His parents,Azure and Wave,there were two strong and loving dolphins.As he told them about his plan,his mother's eyes were filled.Of tears.Blue,are you sure you want to leave? The world beyond the reef is dangerous! Maybe it's just a legend,it is not worth taking such a risk! The father,more detained,nodded.There are dangers that you cannot imagine.Blue looked at his parents with gratitude and spoke to them

gently:
-I have always felt that the reef is only part of our world.I must see what is beyond,I have to discover with my eyes.And his father offered him a final advice:
-Try to follow your instinct,son.The instinct of a dolphin never mistakes.Blue was not alone.He had good friends who were with him at every moment.The closest friend of,Finn,a smaller but extremely dolphin.Intelligent,was the first to ask him:
-You planned everything well? Do you have a route? Do you have energy supplies? You can't leave that way,simply! Blue a laugh.Finn was always the one who analyzed everything in detail.
-I know,Finn.That's why I need your help.One of their friends,Shelly,a large turtle loaded with wisdom,nodded seriously:
-The world beyond the reef is vast and unknown.You have to have healthy energy,to know where to find food and where to shelter.But,above all,you have to take care of the predators.
-Yes,especially sharks! Finn completed.
- They are the masters of the deep waters.Blue remembered the advice and decided to prepare as best as possible.To have energy during the

trip,Blue had to eat well.Delphins feed on small and calm,and Finn helped him find a bank of fresh fish.
-I assure you that you are well fed before you leave! Finn said,following how Blue caught the fish with incredible agility.After eating enough,Blue felt more energetic than ever.He was ready to leave.Admired the bright corals,the multicolored fish that danced through the waters,and the rays of the sun penetrating through the surface of the ocean,creating spectacular light games.At that moment,he felt a goal in the heart.He was ready to leave behind everything he loved.But at the same time,he was prepared for the unknown.
-Take care,Blue! Finn shouted.
-Don't forget about us! Shelly added.Blue smiled,turned to the horizon line,and,with a last look at home,began to drown the adventure of his life.

Chapter 3: The first obstacle

Blue swimming with enthusiasm through the clear waters of the ocean,looking around with curious eyes.Each water waving,every reflection of the solar light that penetrated through the waves brought him a feeling of freedom that he had not experienced until then.He remembered the last words of his mother:
-Take care,Blue! The ocean is bigger than you can imagine,but your brave heart will always guide you.For a while,everything seemed to be well.Turn among the colored fish benches,he greets the sea stars and enjoyed the quiet water breeze.But,at one point,he felt a sudden change in the water current.It was as if an unseen force began to shoot him in an unknown direction.You know how the power of water was increasing more and more,and the swimming became May difficult.

He had begun to encounter resistance to every movement of the swimmers.Blue tried to keep his calm,but the current became more and more powerful.He realized that he had been caught in a marine current,a phenomenon he had heard,but which he had never lived.The shock that he should not fight directly against the current,but try to swim diagonally,so that it is easier to release.But the waves seemed to have other plans for him.As he was worn.For waters,Blue noticed that the surrounding landscape was beginning to change.It did not recognize the coral formations,nor the fish that swam beside him.He had begun to move away from his native reef.The stories of his grandfather who always said:
-A true adventurer is not afraid of the unknown,but wisely confronts him.Inspire to those words,Blue analyzes his options.Maybe they knew how to get rid of this current! With his last forces,he approaches them and shouts:
-Sprinkle me! Can you help me? I was caught in this current and I don't know how to go out! An old turtle,with an algae shell,stopped and looked at him gently.
-You're a brave dolphin,she said.You don't have to resist the current.

Use it to your advantage! If you swim with him for a while,you will find a place to go out without exhausting.Blue listens to the wise advice of the turtle and, instead of fighting the current,began to swim in the same direction,but controlling his movements.After a few minutes that seemed for hours,he noticed how the current was beginning to lose weight.At that time,using his last energy reserves,Blue swims sideways and finally managed to get out of the powerful current.Stop for a moment,breathing deeply and feeling the freedom of his movements again.The old woman followed him from a distance and smiled.
-You have learned an important lesson today,young dolphin.You do not have to fight against the current.Sometimes,you have to use it in your favor.
-Thank you,turtle! I will never forget this advice! The turtle gave him a goodbye and continued his way,and Blue remained in the middle of the quiet waters,feeling more confident than ever.If he was away from home,he had just passed his first obstacle and had learned something valuable.He continued his journey, knowing that many challenges will follow,but with the certainty he was prepared for them.

Chapter 4: Unexpected friendship

Blue advanced cautiously through the unknown waters,feeling alone for the first time.The strong current had removed him from his native reef,and now everything seemed foreigner.The corals had forms he had never seen,the fish were colored differently,and the water had a smell slightly different.Although he was excited about his adventure,a small part of him felt fear.Pluting slowly,heard a short sound,like a sigh.Her carapace was cracked at times,and her small,wise eyes looked at him

gently.
-Who are you, young traveler? asked the tortoise,slowly raising his head.
-I am called Blue,the dolphin said,approaching cautiously.I started on a journey beyond the reef,but the current took me further than I had planned.
-Ah,the ocean always shows you his ways.Isn't it great? My name is Arlo.I crossed these waters more times than you can imagine.
-Then you can help me! I do not know these places well and I do not know how to continue my journey.
-the wisdom of the ocean does not come only from the places you see,but also from the experiences you live.To travel means to learn, to adapt and accept the unknown.At first.
-The first thing you need to know is that the ocean is not a simple road.He is alive,always changing.If you want to continue your journey, you have to learn to read his signs.
-Semns?
Arlo pointed his head toward a bench of silver fish that quickly swam

in a certain direction.

-Do you see those fish? They feel the currents.If you follow them, you can discover safer ways through the water.Also,the changes of the color of the water,the movement of the algae or the sounds you hear can tell you a lot about what follows.To the ocean as in a story he could read.Usually,he just swam where he wanted,but now he understood that he could use these clues to help him.

-Thank you, Arlo! I will remember this advice.The old turtle laughed slightly.

-You are not in a hurry,young.Sphat is just the beginning.Practic makes the difference.Why don't you stay a little here and you don't try to read the ocean? Blue hesitates for a moment,but then accepts.He spent good hours by observing the fish benches,following the movement of water and trying to feel the currents.What time was passing,Blue began to see the ocean with other eyes.It was not just a vast and unknown place,but a space full of clues that could be understood.When the time was to leave,Blue felt a deep gratitude for Arlo.

-I will never forget what you taught me,I promise! Arlo nodded,smiling warmly.

-Then the ocean will be a good friend.Safe,Blue! The dolphin continues its journey,but this time,with a new confidence.The fact that each wave and every current had a story to tell,and he was ready to listen.

Chapter 5: In the footsteps of legends

Blue swam calm down next to Arlo,following every movement of the old turtle.The sunbeans penetrated through the crystalline water,illuminating the blue scales of the young dolphin.Arlo sighed

deeply,as if to share a well -kept secret.He stopped on a reef covered with algae and looked at the horizon.
 -Have you ever heard of the lost town of Corals? Arlo asked in a low,mysterious voice.Balue blinked curiously.
 -The lost? Sounds ... Fantastic! What is it? The turtle smiled,glancing with wisdom.
- It is more than a story.It was a real place,a submerged fortress where the corals were growing in unmoved forms,and the creatures of the sea lived in peace and harmony.It is said that it was protected by an old spirit of the ocean,which kept away the dangers.But one day,the city was swallowed by water and no one has ever found it.Blue gave his tail several times,intrigued.
 -No one? No one at all?
-I say they have seen the ruins,others I think it's just a legend,said Arlo.But I know one thing for sure:this place exists,and in its depths there is something precious.Delfin is closer,his big and curious eyes reflecting the blue light of the ocean.
-Something precious? How do you mean? Arlo stretched his paws and drew in the fine sand a strange symbol,similar to a bright sun.

-It is said that in the heart of the city,hidden among corals and caves,there is a gold coral,a legendary artifact that has the power to bring balance into the ocean.
-The golden body? And you think it's true?
-I do not know for sure,Arlo said.But the legends do not appear out of nothing.If you are determined to explore the ocean,to know that this could be your biggest adventure.Delfin thought for a moment.Tempting,but he knew it couldn't be easy.
-How could i find it? Blue asked.
-This is the heavy part.No one knows exactly where he is,but I heard stories about three indications that lead to him.Blue feels a thrill of emotion.
-Those indications? The turtle nodded.
-The first indication is in a crystal cave,where the winds of the wind sing the stories of the past.The second is hidden among the dance algae forests,where the moonlight draws maps.And third...no one knows exactly,but it is said that it is said Only those with a pure heart can discover it.Blue gave the tail,impatient.
-This sounds...incredible! Do you think I could find the lost city? Arlo looked at him seriously.
-You have courage,Blue,and a clean heart.But such a journey is not without danger.The dark water hides many unknowns.The Delfin thought of the strong currents,the unseen predators of the ocean and how far he was.But something in him pushed him forward,a longing for the unknown that he had never felt.
-I must try! he said determined.
-Then,the first step is to find the crystal cave.It is said that it is south of the shadow reef,beyond the silver sand plains.Blue felt a wave of

emotion.It had never been so far,but now it had a purpose.
-Thank you,Arlo! I'll be back with news about the city! The turtle shook his head with a wise smile.
-Be careful,little.The ocean is beautiful,but also dangerous.Where he had met Arlo.As far as he was swimming,his thoughts flew to what would discover.The legends were true? If the lost city really existed,what would he find there? He didn't know the answers yet, but one thing was sure: his adventure had just begun.

Chapter 6: Meeting with shark

Blue swam with speed through the endless waters of the ocean,following the direction of Arlo.Around him,the sand on the bottom of the sea seemed to stretch like a silver canvas,and the sun's rays were reflected in the light waves above.It had not been Never far from home,but every beat of the tail increased his enthusiasm.He was approaching an area where the reef became more and more rare,and the depths seemed to stretch like an unknown gap.Here,in this deserted place,the quiet it seemed strange.It was quiet.Suddenly,a cold chill was passing through the swimmers.He felt that he was not alone.A vague sound,like a whisper in the water,made him turn his eyes.But then,from the depths,two yellow eyes appeared,fixed on him.A shark! Blue felt his heart beat more.The huge crease was slowly approaching,with almost hypnotic movements.His gray was melted with dark waters,and his dorsal swimmer cut as a blade.
-Well,what do we have here? He said the shark in a low,serious voice.A lonely dolphin,so far from home.Blue swallowed dry and try to look calm.
-I'm just passing,he said,trying to keep his voice firm.

-Pass? Through my territory? he asked,smiling slightly,which revealed his ranks of sharp teeth.I don't think so.
-My name is a razor,said the predator,narrowing his eyes.And I don't like it when strangers walk through my waters without permission.
-I didn't want to disturb anyone,Blue assures,trying to keep their calm.I was looking for the crystal cave.Razor's eyes glittered for a moment.
-The crystal peanut? he repeats.Well,this is interesting.What does the job have such a small dolphin with such a mysterious place? Blue hesitates.He wasn't sure if he had to tell the truth.If the shark knew more about the cave? But at the same time,if he lied to him,he could have upset him even harder.
-I want to find the lost city of the corals,Blue admitted.
-The lost? Ha! A story for the dreamy fish.There is no such thing.Blue frowns.
-We exist! I heard stories about him.If I find the crystal cave,I can discover clues to take me there.
-You know...maybe you really believe in stories,little.But the ocean is not a place for dreams.It's a place for survivors.It was dangerous,that was clear.But something in his voice suggested that he knew more

than he could see.
-Have you ever been there? Blue asked with courage.The raveer remained silent for a moment,then turned his eyes.
-I was in many places,he said.I learned that beautiful things came with a price.Those words made Blue wonder if the shark had ever been looking for the city.But he had no time to continue his thoughts,because,In a moment,Razor suddenly turned to him, approaching himself threateningly.
-But enough talk.Now,what to do with you? Blue feels how adrenaline invades his body.If he did not go out quickly from this situation,he could become the prey of the shark.He thought quickly.What could he do? Then an idea came to him.
-You know, Razor,he said slowly,I heard that those who find the lost city are considered the masters of the ocean.But...If you think it's just a legend,you are probably not interested.
-The masters of the ocean? Blue nodded.
-Yes.It is said that anyone who finds the city and the golden coral becomes the strongest in the sea.The raler narrows their eyes.
-And do you think you could do that? Blue shrugged,trying to look confident.
-Maybe.But if you do not believe in him,you probably have no reason to be worried.
-Hmph.You have courage,dolphin.But do not think you escaped.The ocean did not forgive the weak.And,with those words,the razor turned and moved away,disappearing again in the shadows of the water.Feeling his heart beating strongly.He had escaped.But at the same time...he had managed to get something precious:Razor believed more in the legend than he recognized.With a last sigh of relief,Blue continues his way.This adventure became more and more dangerous.

Chapter 7: Dark caves

Blue slowly swimming,leaving behind the endless stretch of the open ocean and approaching an area where the sea began to become injured.The huge stones rose like imposing walls,and the dark entrances of underwater caves were in front of him.Some mouths that promised the unknown.In front of him there was a maze of underwater tunnels,whom old Arlo had told him to hide hundreds of years old.Out of the dark.Blue took a moment of breath and looked around.And slipped into the main cave.Inside,the darkness immediately wrapped it.The stone breeds were covered by algae and fossilized coral,and sometimes,a few small fish were running in front of it,scared of the presence of a stranger.Through the water.The reunications were back,drawing in his mind a contour of the tunnel.He was in a narrow passage,but as he went,the cave became wider,like a huge room hidden underwater.At one point, something shine weakly in the wall.Blue approached curiously and observed some ancient inscriptions.They were deeply dug in and partially covered by sediments and algae.They approached more and studying them carefully.It was a symbol that resembled a spiral,followed by an arrow what seemed to indicate the depths.

-Those who seek the gold of the corals must follow the path where the light does not penetrate.Blue frown.What could that mean? Continuing its exploration,it swims deeper into the tunnel.As it was approaching a new opening,you felt a change in the water.A cold wind,like an invisible breath,seemed to come out of a dark hole in the rocky wall.Continues its way and discovered another inscription,more detailed.This depicted a rudimentary map of the tunnels,and in the center was a drawing

of a bright coral.
-In the heart of darkness,the treasures of the lost will light the way.Blue was trying to understand what this message meant when a strange sound caught his attention.Somewhere in the dark,something moved.Easy,as if something slid down the walls.Sometimes,two pairs of yellow eyes lit up in the dark.Blue was instinctively back.From the shadow,two gigantic fish came out,covered with black scales and sharp teeth.
-Intrus ...said one of them in a low,hoarse voice.
-What are you looking for here? asked the other,swimming slowly around him.Blue tried to keep his calm.
-I do not want trouble,he said.I only have clues about the lost city of the corals.The people looked between them,then laughed briefly.
-You go further,little,said first.But you know that from these caves are not all back.Of something important.He was in a huge underwater room,where the ceiling seemed to disappear in the dark.Here,the walls were covered with layers of fossilized coral,and in the center of the room a large,smooth stone.Different from the others.And he notices

that the stone had a small opening in the middle. A key? A mechanism? Curious, he stretched his muzzle and gently blows water over her. Something, something moved. Under the layers of time, it became visible. It was the image of a huge, golden coral, surrounded by waves and unknown marine creatures. Above it, a symbol was engaged that Blue had never seen: a circle surrounded by small rays, as a star of the depths. Blue feels the emotion encompasses it. This was a hint! A sign that the lost city of Corals was not just a myth! But before he could analyze better, a deafening noise sounded through tunnels. And fast! With his heart beating strongly, he used all his speed and swim to the exit, avoiding pieces of rock that collapsed around him. The tunnel became more and more narrow, but at the last moment, he found a crack in the wall and slipped out exactly when he slipped out exactly when he slipped out exactly when he slipped out exactly A huge stone wall collapsed behind him. They said deeply, trying to recover. He had escaped. But more importantly, he had discovered a real hint about the lost city of the corals. With the heart full of emotion, Blue looked up to the horizon. He was going to continue the adventure, more determined than ever.

Chapter 8: Test of courage

Blue was floating in the middle of an underwater room bathed in the dark. The heart was beating quickly, still feeling the echo of the danger he had gone through. The tunnel he had crossed had collapsed behind him, blocking any way back. Now, in front of him, the only one The way out was a narrow tunnel, so dark that not even his ecolocation was able to outline him completely. He was afraid. The cold water of the water

caressed his swimmers,and his thoughts were crammed into his mind. -If I block me? If I run out of air? What if something dangerous is waiting for me in the tunnel? He remembered the stories he had heard about the explorers of the seas that ventured into unknown places and about some who never returned.But then he remembered something else.To give up now.He had to be brave.They said deeply,filling his lungs with air,and approved of the entrance of the tunnel.As he swam in the tunnel,Blue felt the space became more and more tight.Fossilized and sharp rocky formations.He had to control his movements perfectly,not to hit and not lose precious time.When,in time,thin currents of cold water made him tremble,and the outside sounds seemed to disappear completely.He could hear it was his own breath and heartbeat.He tried to use his ecolocation to see how long the tunnel was,but the sounds were chaotic,making him not be able to figure out the road.Part of him wanted to return.But he had no place.He carefully,trying to keep his calm.At one point,he felt a sudden movement in the water.He stopped instinctively.From the dark,something was slowly approaching.A small,dark silhouette was moving on the walls.Blue held his breath.The creed showed his shape, a flashlight,with a bright globe that hung in front of him,pulsing in the dark. Blue sighed.It was not a danger,but the meeting was giving him.A few seconds,then swim further,leaving behind small bright particles.The delphin thought about how beautiful,but also dangerous the world of the depths.But he had no time to admire the landscape.The tunnel seemed to become even narrower.The critical moment.While advanced,Blue felt the walls of the tunnel slightly touches his skin.There was no room to swim freely.He had to slip carefully,moving slowly to hurt.Carefully,but at a At the moment,part of the fossilized coral collapsed suddenly next to him,lifting a cloud of dust.Balue frightened and made a sudden movement.You feel a sharp pain at the right swimming.He had hit a sharp corner of the stone.The pain was bearable,But the danger was another,the cloud of high stone dust began to fill the tunnel,completely reducing its visibility.Blue began to feel his breath.He was caught in a tight space,in the dark,without seeing where he went.Exactly the kind of situation that was most afraid of.But he had to keep his calm.He remembered Arlo's advice:

-When you are in a difficult situation,stop. Don't let the panic control you.Launches a sound signal and listens carefully to the echo.This time,he managed to detect a greater opening in front,a few meters.He was almost.He concentrated all his will and swim before,carefully slipping through the stones.With each meter The light began to become more visible.After a few moments that seemed to him an eternity,he suddenly felt a different current.The tunnel was widening.Blue realized that he was reaching out.Outside the tunnel,in a larger cave,where the weak light of the ocean managed to penetrate.They stirred deeply,leaving himself enveloped in the feeling of freedom.Fears,with doubt and panic.Now,he felt that he was stronger.Around,Blue noticed that the cave had a direct exit to the ocean. He was just beginning.

Chapter 9: Unexpected help

Blue was floating quietly in the light lighted by the sun's filtered rays.He had been from the narrow tunnel,but it was not completely safe.It was in an unknown place,and the route to the ocean was not clear.They were slowly rotating,researching the surroundings.

-How do I get out of here? Blue was asked.His disgust was not discovered any obvious output.The cave was closed from all sides.He had started to feel a slight fear again.If he was stuck here? He slowly headed to the walls of the cave,looking for a hidden passage.But everything seemed solid.Just when he was beginning to feel despair,a small bright point in the darkness caught his attention.A small,translucent fish,with a bright globe on his forehead.And warm,like stars.Blue looked at him with astonishment.Delfin looked at them fascinated.He had never seen such creatures so close.He understood the message.They guided him to the exit.He slowly after them,following their hypnotic dance.The people seemed to know exactly where to go, avoiding any obstacle.At the beginning,Blue hesita.He had never met such creatures and did not know if he could trust them.But then he remembered the lessons learned in his journey.Sometimes,the help comes from the most unexpected places.So he left his fear aside and allowed himself to be guided.Of the cave where,at first glance,there was no exit.But,as he approached,Blue observes a narrow crack between the rocks,hidden in the shadows.You can swim directly through it,illuminating the way.Blue approaches the opening and He inspired deep.

-If I block me? What if it's the wrong road? he thought for a moment. But then he looked at the fish bench,waiting for him beyond the crack, pulsing slightly in golden light. They were not scared. Soon, the space began to widen. Then, suddenly, he woke up in a magnificent underwater tunnel, where the walls were covered with phosphorescent corals, and the water was clear and lively. The fish stopped for a moment, as if he wanted to make sure that Blue sees the exit. The delphin thanked them. Then, with a last pulse of light, the fish dispersed, turning into their fish. In the ocean. Blue swims with power to the light. A few seconds later, went out into a lagoon bathed in the sun, where the crystalline water caressed his skin and where he could breathe again the fresh air of the sea. You feel a deep gratitude. Without the help of the-light fish, maybe it would never have found the exit. This experience had shown him an important thing: you are never alone, even in the darkest places. With a new wave, Blue He turned his eyes off.

Chapter 10: Hurricane

Blue swam quietly through the clear waters of the ocean, admiring the dance of the sunshine that pierced the surface of the water. After the attempts he had gone through, the dark tunnel, the meeting with the fish-fish and all the previous obstacles,he felt for the first time a deep silence.But this peace did not it would last.Suddenly,he felt a change in the water.A unnatural coolness encompassed him,and the surrounding currents began to shake.Blue looked up to the surface and observed something worrying: the black clouds covered the sky,and the sunlight seemed to gradually disappear.You feel an increasing anxiety in the chest.Then,a troubled fish passed by it,swimming frantically in the opposite direction.

-Run! A storm comes! cries the fish without stopping.Balue tense.A storm? He had never been trapped in such a powerful,but he had heard stories about the ocean whisper,destroying everything in their path.If this was one of those storms,he had to find a shelter, and quickly! The waves in the distance became bigger,and the currents pushed his body in an unwanted direction.The water seemed to have caught life,moving in a chaotic,uncontrolled way.Blue began to swim against the current,trying to approach a reef where he hoped to find a safe place.But the strong wind above had already lifted huge waves,and the whole sea had become a dangerous place.People and other marine creatures were running in all directions,looking for shelter.

More overwhelming.He had to find a place to hide before it was too late! Swimming with all the power,Blue remembered a place that Arlo had described,the wise turtle.

-If you will ever be caught by a storm,look for shelter in coral reefs! There the waves do not have the same force,and the currents are weaker! The reefs! This was his only chance.Trying to ignore the strength of the wind that felt even in the water,Blue advanced to a chain of reefs a few miles away.But as the storm was approaching,the waves became higher and taller lifting it and throwing it strongly.For the first time on its journey,he felt a real fear.The glow lighting the dark sky,sending ghost reflections in the water.The tunnels rang so hard that they seemed to shake the whole ocean.And Blue had to be extremely careful not to get caught in them.A huge wave came from behind,and before he could react,the water force pushed him down.He rolled,losing his orientation.Around him,around him The water had become a mixture of sand and white foam,and he did not know in what direction the surface was and in what direction the bottom of the ocean was.

-Don't panic! he thought.Breathe! Find a landmark! He used his ecolocation and managed to detect the form of the reefs not far from him.He was desperately to them,while the waves continued to push him.Louder.Inside the reef,the waters were still agitated,but at least they did not pull it in all directions.They settled near a wall of corals and regained their breath.He had to shelter...but the storm was far from over.They continued to hit the reef,and the sounds of the thunder rang like frightening bubbles.Alleges and coral fragments were torn by powerful currents,and Blue could feel the whole of the sea.Around him,other marine creatures were hiding in the cracks of the reef:A bench of colorful fish had been hidden under a coral arc,and a octopus stuck to a stone,trying not to be snatched.The ocean,his house,could be gentle, and scary. The time seemed to have stopped in place. Blue didn't know how long, maybe minutes, maybe. Of violence, and the lightning became more and more rare. Finally, the sky began to light again. Blue looked up and saw the first rays of the clouds. He had disappeared. Blue left his shelter and carefully swim through the reefs. Many of the corals had been destroyed, and the sand on the bottom of the sea was disturbed. But the life of the ocean was already beginning to move again. A bench of brave fish had left their hiding. Turtle slowly swims next to him, looking at the clear sky above. The ocean had survived the storm.

Chapter 11: The secret island

When the ocean calmed down after the devastating storm, Blue felt he had to continue his journey. He still felt his tired muscles because of the struggle with strong waves, but he was grateful. He had survived again in the sky, and the water, although cloudy, He was beginning to regain his silence. While swimming further, he felt a gentle girlfriend in the water, a different current, which urged him to follow him. Without being too thinking, Blue used his instincts and began to move to the unknown. After a few hours of swimming, a mysterious island was outlined. Although Blue had seen many reefs and rocky formations on his journey, this place was different. It was surrounded by blue and clear waters, and on the bottom of the sea were seen corals in vibrant colors. As it was approaching, it saw silhouettes that moved agile through the water. Dolphin! But they were not like the people of his native reef. Blue slows the movements and approaches with caution. A group of elegant and larger dolphins than he swam in circles, communicating through melodious sounds. They were on guard, and one of them, one Gray-silver dolphin with penetrating eyes, swim to meet him.

-Who are you and what are you looking for on our island? asked the foreign dolphin with a firm tone.Balue felt a thrill of restlessness,but he gathers his courage.

-I call me Blue.I was caught in a storm and,following the currents,I arrived here.I didn't know there was such a beautiful island and ... a colony of unknown dolphins! The surrounding dolphins slammed each other,analyzing it with curious eyes.

-We are the lunar dolphins.This insulating is our house for generations,and no one from outside has arrived here.Other members of the colony.Blue notices that they were all bigger and faster than ordinary dolphins.They had slightly silver skin,and during the night they said that their skin was glowing weakly under the moonlight,a rarely encountered phenomenon.A older dolphin,With scars on the sides,swim toward him.

-I am Elder Kairo,the leader of this colony.You found it by chance,but maybe the ocean wanted our roads to intersect.Tell me,Blue, where do you come from and what is the purpose of your trip? Blue told them all:about his native reef,about his desire to explore the unknown and about the legend of the lost city of the corals he had told.

-The lost coral...Elder Kairo murmured.

This is an old legend,but it is said that some indications about his existence could be hidden near our island.

-Serious? Have you heard of him too?

-Of course,but few are the ones who had the courage to look for him.There are great dangers,and many who started on this trip did not return.This was not the first time Blue heard about the risks of searching for this legendary city,But this time you felt a weight in the words of the old dolphin.After the discussion with Elder Kairo,Blue was invited to explore the island.It was an amazing place,the reefs around the island were the most beautiful he had ever seen,full of phosphorescent corals,fish exotic and hidden caves.A group of young dolphins in the colony guided him through the hidden lagoons and showed him something truly fascinating: old inscriptions on underwater rocks,which seemed to tell a story.

-Yes are written old legends about the ocean. It is said that in the past,our dolphins protected a great treasure,but it was lost in the depths.No one knows where they are really...Blue looked fascinating the symbols engraved in stone.They seemed familiar to them,similar to the ones he had seen in the dark fish.Did this colony hide an important indication about the location of the Corals lost? Before the sunset,Elder Kairo calls Blue again.

-In order to be considered a friend of monthly dolphins,you must prove that you are worthy of our confidence.

-How can i do that? Blue asked,feeling a challenge.

-No,lunar dolphins,we are known for our speed and agility.We want to see if you have the courage to compete in a swimming test with one of our best swimmers.Big and more quick than him,but he could not refuse this chance.

-I accept the challenge! he said determined.Thus,in the light of the West,Blue was preparing for the most important race in his life.If he managed to gain the respect of the monthly dolphins,he can discover a new secret about the legend of the Corals.

Chapter 12: The ancient secrets

Blue had managed to earn the respect of monthly dolphins after accepting their challenge.It had not been easy,but his courage and determination helped him prove his value.Now,surrounded by his new friends,he was preparing to find out one of the best kept secrets of the ocean.After the acceptance ceremony,Elder Kairo led him into an underwater cave between the rocks of the island.The teaching was narrow and dark,but once they entered,an amazing show was revealed to Blue.The ropes were covered with ancient inscriptions,glittering weakly in the thunder of water.In the middle of the room,a coral statue appeared a dolphin with wings engraved with unknown symbols.
-This is one of the most sacred places of monthly dolphins,said Elder Kairo.Here the secrets of the ocean,transmitted from generation to generation,slowly swim around the room,admiring the mysterious beauty of the cave.
-What does these inscriptions mean? he asked,fascinated.A old dolphin,who seemed to be the history of the colony,approached and began to explain.
-These symbols speak of a magic artifact,known as the pearl of time.It is said that this artifact protects the ocean and its natural balance.
-A magic artifact? Elder Kairo nodded.
- Legend has it that this pearl was created by the ocean thousands of years ago,to maintain the harmony between its creatures.He wanted

to use it for selfish purposes.

-When are he now? Blue asked eagerly.The old woman sighed.

-We do not know exactly.But it is believed that the clues to find the pearl of time are hidden in the lost city of the corals.Blue feels how the heart beats faster.Now,he discovered that that place was hiding an even greater secret,a magic artifact that could protect the entire ocean.

-If this artifact is so important,why has it not found it so far? Blue asked.Elder Kairo looked at him seriously.

-Many creatures have sought it over time,but the road is full of dangers.It is said that only a brave and pure soul can find the way to the pearl of time.Discover this legendary artifact? After leaving the sacred cave,Blue and Elder Kairo withdrew at sea,looking at the moon reflected on the surface of the water.

-What will you do now,Blue? asked the old dolphin.Blue had no doubt.

-I will continue the journey.If the pearl of time is in the lost city of the corals,I have to find it.Not only for me,but for the whole ocean.Elder Kairo smiled approvingly.

-You have a brave soul,my young friend.But you know that you will need more than courage.He needed wisdom,patience and trust allies.

-Before you leave,there is something else you have to see.Elder Kairo led him to another part of the island,where a huge,golden coral was growing at the bottom of the sea.
-It is said that this coral was once touched by the magic of the pearl of time.Those who touch it can feel connected with the ocean and can find out if they are meant to follow the path to Artifact.Of the coral.A wave of heat crossed it and,for a fraction of a second, had a vision:a submerged coral fortress,a dazzling light and a threatening shadow that was approaching.When the vision ended,Blue remained still,breathing deep.Elder Kairo looked at him carefully.
-You saw something,didn't you? Blue nodded slowly.
-Yes. I think...I think I saw the lost city of the corals.Elder Kairo closed his eyes for a moment,then spoke in a serious voice.
-Then your destiny is clear.You have to go to that place.But you take care,because where there are treasures,there are dangers.Blue looks up to the starry sky.

Chapter 13: The road to Abis

Blue swam through the clear waters,leaving the secret island with an undeniable determination.His reason was clear:to find the pearl of time.But to reach the lost city of the corals,he had to go through unknown places.To the oceanic abyss,a place that few had visited and from where fewer had returned.It was a mysterious territory,where the sunlight did not penetrate,and strange creatures made its way through the shadows.As it went down,Blue felt the water temperature it gradually decreased.The living chickens of the reef remained behind,replaced by darker tones of blue and black.Around him, he ocean became silent,and the only sounds were the beats of his wings and a few distant echoes of other marine creatures.

-I did I make the right choice? Blue thought,but immediately chasing his doubts.He had to continue,no matter what to discover. After a few hours of swimming,Blue met a strange phenomen hot.The black smokers,as Arlo once told them,were hydrothermal mouths that released gases from the depths.Balue approached carefully,feeling the increasing water.From one of the cracks,a huge fish,covered with silver scales and sharp teeth,he looked at him for a moment,then disappeared in the dark.

-Now no one is friendly,Blue thought,continuing his way.After leaving his fumarole,Blue felt a strong current,which attracted him to an underwater tunnel.In the depths.A little lane-fish,who swam near,looked at him scared.

-Run!, before they pull you too! Blue shone with all the strength,but the current became more and more powerful.It was caught in what the elders called "the wind of the abyss",a force that was pulling everything in the ocean's depths.Despite his efforts,Blue was pulled into the whirlwind and he felt the darkness swallowing it.Blue felt without control.He was chaotic,trying to find a support point, but it was as if he had fallen into the empty.Strange creatures,with big eyes and huge teeth,floated through the darkness, attracted by his movements.Blue knew that the abyss was dangerous,but he had not imagined he would be so hostile.When he thought everything was lost,Blue noticed a dim light.But constant,in the distance.He turned to her,following the instinct.He was closer,he discovers that the light came from a huge cave,with walls covered by bright corals.Blue sighed relieved.He stated by the wind of the abyss.In front of him stretched something incredible:the ruins of an ancient city,covered by marine vegetation and phosphorescent corals.He felt that he had discovered something important,but he still didn't know what dangers they were waiting for.While swimming among the ruins,Blue noticed a strange inscription on a stone wall.Before he could understand something,a huge shadow slipped behind him.He was not alone in the abyss.

Chapter 14: The monster in the depths

Still disturbed by the steep descent into the abyss,Blue held his breath when he felt the huge shadow approaching.The heart was beating his chest.He was turning,preparing for any danger.A colossal shape floated among the ruins of the sunken city.It raised as a monster of legends:a long,muscular body,huge tentacles that were slowly and a huge mouth,full of sharp teeth.Make no movement.If the monster saw him,he had no chance to escape.But the creature did not seem to have observed it.Slowly through the water,gently touching the ruins with his long tentacles,as if he were looking for something.Blue felt a strange sensation of sadness coming from the creature.It did not seem angry or aggressive.Rather it seemed...alone.The curiosity was stronger than fear,so Blue was moving slightly before,approaching a little.When he made this gesture,one of the tentacles,and The big eyes of the creature fastened on it.Blue froze.But instead of attacking,the monster blinked slowly and made a deep,guttural sound.A sound that does not express anger,but wonder.

-You are not like the others...said the creature suddenly,in a low,but gentle voice.

-Who...Who are you? the dolphin asked,with an uncertain voice.The creed waved his tentacles and approaches slightly,without seeming threatening.

-I am Nox.and who are you,the little stranger? Blue gathers his courage and swims a little closer.

-I call me Blue.I have the pearl of time.I arrived here by mistake,drawn by currents.

-And you are a seeker of legends,like the others.

-What do you mean? What happened to others? Nox closed his eyes for a moment,as if overwhelmed with memories.

-Long ago,a group of explorers came to this place.They were something important.But,they were thirsty for power,they tried to take treasures

that did not belong to them.The ocean was not gentle with them.And the shadows swallowed them.Since then,no one left here...Blue felt a cold thrill.
-And you? How did you get here?
"Me?" Nox sighed.
-I didn't choose to be here.I was left behind.Blue realized that Nox wasn't a monster.It was just a single creature,forgotten by the world.
-You were abandoned? Blue asked,sad.
-Yes...long ago.Those like me were afraid of other creatures.They said we were dangerous.So they drove me in the depths.Since then, I stayed here.Blue realized that,although it was small and vulnerable in comparison With nox,they had something in common:the desire to belong to a place.
-I don't think you're dangerous,Nox.Just that no one really knew you.Nox looked at him surprised.
-You are the first to tell me this.Blue now swims relaxed near Nox.He had begun to see the creature not as a monster,but as a possible ally.
-Maybe you can help me,Nox.caet the pearl of time.It is said that it is in the lost city of the corals.At the hearing of these words,Nx's eyes narrowed slightly.
-The time of time...I heard about it.But she is guarded by something more frightening than me.
-What do you mean?
-the shafts of the depths.They protect the treasure.And they will not let anyone take it easily.Delfin felt a mixture of fear and enthusiasm.His adventure was just beginning.But now,he had an unexpected ally:a colossus of the depths,a "monster "Which was not what seemed to be.
-Will you help me? Blue asked,hopefully in the voice.Nox remained

silent for a moment,in a determined voice,said:
-Yes. But we have to be prepared.

Chapter 15: Facing the pearls thieves

Blue swam next to Nox,the colossus of the depths,following the route marked by the ancient corals.
-You are you? whispered Blue.Nox slowly waving his tentacles,tasting the water with his fine senses.
-Yes.We are not alone.Delfin swallowed in the century since he had been looking for the pearl of time,he had learned that this treasure was coveted by many creatures of the ocean.But who would dare to penetrate so deep? Suddenly,an ink cloud darkens the water.Blue was instinctively tugs back,but it was already surrounded.Find huge octopuses appeared in the shadows.They had small, wicked eyes,and their suction cups seemed full of scars.Their lider,A reddish octopus with a missing eye,undertakes its tentacles with arrogance.
-What do we have here? he growled.A dolphin and a monster.I heard that you hunt the pearl of time.But we have bad news for you:

the pearl belongs to us.

-Therla does not belong to anyone! Protect the ocean! The boss laughed thickly.

-Exact.And if we have it,we can control who lives and who perishes.The other cucumbers chuckled and twisted their threatening tentacles.

-We will not let you take it! Blue said,trying to look brave.Nox was moving forward,and his colossal presence made the water tremble.

-They now and you will not suffer.But the pearl thieves did not seem impressed.Their lider whispered:

-To! Blue was away at the last moment,avoiding the tentacles that rushed toward him.Nox opened his arms and hit hard,causing two octopuses to rolled into the water.But the thieves were agile and experienced.Blue quickly realized that the direct fight was not the best strategy.Characrats could change their color and disappear in the environment,attacking the shadow.He had to think quickly. He remembered the reefs with narrow caves he had seen.

-Nox,follow me! shout Blue.Delfin swims quickly to massive corals,slipping among tight openings.As he hoped,the octopus followed. Blue knew an old trick of dolphins:he could create high frequency sounds.Area full of rocks and crammed corals,began to make clicks and intense sounds.The characters were shaking.He used his colossal force:he pushed a massive rock,blocking the exit of the pearls.The characters struggled,but they had nowhere to run.

-You got it,dolphin! But don't think I'm done with you! Blue swam in front of them with a confident smile.

-The this as a lesson:the ocean does not belong to the greedy.

-He could finally go out,Nox said,but they will have time to think about their mistakes.Blue and Nx left the area,heading for the sinking city.

-You were brave,Nox said.You thought quickly.You did what many would not have succeeded.Blue smiled,but he knew that the challenges had not ended here.In front of them,the pearl of time was waiting for them...but other unknown dangers.

Chapter 16.Blue and the pearl of time

Blue was floating in the middle of the quiet waters,looking with emotion to the ancient cave in front of him.After the exhausting confrontation with the pearl thieves,the five cunning octopuses that used the black ink to hide,the little dolphin felt the fatigue pressing his swimmers.That he was so close to the pearl of time gave him power.This pearl,about which the old dolphins were talking with reverence,was a legendary artifact,capable of maintaining the balance of the ocean and connecting the past with the future.The pearl of time seemed to be detached from Another world.The entry was covered by long curtains of phosphorescent algae,which were slowly waving in the gentle current,creating a hypnotic effect.In the inside,the walls were decorated with ancient inscriptions,carefully carved by the generations of dolphins

Engravings were talking about a forgotten era,about mythical creatures and the protection that the pearl of time offered the oceans.Blue advanced with caution,still feeling in the water the traces of the ink scattered by the malicious octopus.These creatures had tried to steal the pearl for their own goals,but the little dolphin He had managed to face them and drive them away.Now,in front of him was an underwater cathedral,a wide room with coral columns and marine stone stalactites,which shone weakly in the light filtered by the deep waters.In the middle of the room,on a pedestal Covered with bright corals,was the pearl of time.This was a perfect sphere,bigger than any pearl ever seen,emanating a gentle,silver aura.As a Blue was approaching,the pearl seemed to pulsate slightly,as if he had his own life.Her warm lumina filled the whole cave,causing the inscriptions on the walls to look live.Blue felt her heart beating with power.She had understood that this pearl could not be taken by anyone.They had tried,but only those with a clean heart would he could raise without the magic of the place breaking down.He remembered the wise lessons of the old dolphins,who had told him that the pearl of time was not only a relic,but a symbol of the harmony of the ocean.At that moment,a gentle light was enveloping him,and a wave of sensations overwhelm him.For a few seconds,he felt he was connected to the whole ocean.Imagini of the past and future were lighting through his mind,vast and endless seas,creatures that had once ruled On the waters,the future of his reef and the marine world.Then,everything calm down.Blue raises the pearl and,to his surprise,the cave did not collapse,as he feared.A hidden road, carved by waters in the walls of the cave.It seemed that the pearl of time had recognized his pure intentions and opened his path.The dolphin was a wave of emotion growing in it.He was aware of his responsibility now.

A magic object, but a symbol of wisdom and protection. The old dolphin had explained that the power of this pearl should not be used for selfish purposes, but to maintain the balance of the ocean. With the decision, exit the cave, with the pearl shining slightly at his neck, for his neck that the brilliant pearl was linked to a bright blue pulsing marine plant. The surrounding peppers seemed to light up as it was, as if the ocean itself recognized the importance of its mission. Blue had to reach the old dolphins to fully understand the power. Which he now wore around his neck. As he approached the secret reef where the old dolphins lived, his thoughts were full of questions. What would he learn about the pearl? How could he use it to protect the ocean? He knew this adventure was not the end, but just the beginning of a bigger trip.

Chapter 17: The teaching of the elderly

Blue swam with an impatient heart to the secret island, carrying both the victory over the thieves and the weight of the new artifact. Dolphins of the colony were waiting for him in silence. They had settled in a perfect circle, like the waves that spread in a quiet sea. In the middle of them,

the wisest of them,Elder Solis,looked at him with deep and gentle eyes.
-You managed to bring the artifact.But do you know what that means,Blue? The young dolphin felt that all eyes were pointing to him.
-I know it is a powerful object...but I do not understand how I can use it.Elder Solis nodded.
-Then,it's time to learn.Balue was driven in a large cave,surrounded by ancient drawings in the walls.These showed scenes with dolphins,sharks,oceans and other creatures,but they all seemed to a glittering light,without doubt,the pearl.
-Now thousands of years,the ocean was a chaos,Elder Solis began.The currencies collapsed in each other,the reefs disappeared under the waves,and the creatures of the sea lived in fear.Blue listened fascinated, watching the drawings.
-Then,the first guardians of the waters found this pearl,a gift from the depths.It was a relic that could harmonize the waves and control the currents,but only if it was used wisely.To the throat.
-So does that? Control the ocean? Solis smiled,but he had a serious look.
-No,Blue.Not controls the ocean.He listens and balances it.To prove his power,the elders led Blue at sea,to a place where the currents collided,forming dangerous whirlwinds.
-This is your first test,Solis said.He learns to feel the ocean,not force him.Blue looked down.The water was chaotic,and the thought of entering there made his heart beat faster.
-Do I have to swim there?
-Yes! and tried to feel her vibrations.At first,nothing changes.But then,very slowly,something from the depths seemed to whisper.A rhythmic pulsation.With him...slowly,he adjusted his swimming.

Instead of fighting the current,he was carried for a moment,listening to the vibrations of the water.And then,with a small pulp,he sent a light wave through the pearl.The old people were watching remotely and nodded.Blue came to the surface,breathing hard,but with eyes shining with emotion.
-I succeed! Solis approves with a smile.
-It is just the beginning,Blue.But you took the first step to understand the true power of the pearl of time.

Chapter 18: Return home

Blue swam speed to his native reef,excited and excited.After so many adventures,after so many lessons learned,he was finally returning home.He missed his family,his friends who had seen him on his full journey.Of the ocean was playing through the waves, and the sun's rays penetrated deeply,illuminating the multicolored corals.Everything seemed the same as the day he had left.But as he approached,you felt something.They were moving agitated,and the reef,once lively,seemed immersed in an unnatural silence.Fishermen.Hidden among the corals and looked carefully.In the water,huge nets were thrown,and the fish benches were desperately struggling in an attempt to escape.The one of his dolphins were trying to release the caught life,but they were powerless in the face of danger dimension.Blue felt like a cold rage encompasses him.The people did not understand that the reef was their house? With a tight heart,they continued their way to the cave where he had grown.His mother,Azure,was there,along with other dolphins from the reef.She saw,her eyes filled with tears of joy.

-Blue! You've come back! He rubs his muzzle of hers with affection.

-Mom, what's going on?

-The people came a few days ago.They are in place everywhere and destroy the corals with their anchors.It is not long until our reef is completely destroyed...Blue looks around.All the creatures seemed scared.The octopuses,even the small shrimp who used to tickle him on the tail,everyone was hiding from the terror of the nets.He knew he had to do something.Blue thought of all the lessons he had learned on his journey.Balancing the ocean,but could these people stop? He remembered what Elder Solis had said:

-Do not control the ocean,listen to him.

If he could use the pearl to attract the powerful currents of the sea,maybe he could have chased the boats! He got up in the middle of the dolphin group and said:
-We must work together! We will use the power of currents and waves to make people leave.Delfini watched each other,hesitating.
-But, Blue? They are too strong...said one of them.
-I think I have to use the artifact was thinking Blue.But when he looked at the throat,the pearl of time was not visible,and in Blue's mind a voice said:
-I must deposit me in the oceanic sanctuary,here I have no power.They cannot be used for personal purposes.

Chapter 19: Salvation plan

Blue was floating above the reef,looking down to the beauty of his world.The colorful collars,the fish that danced among the waves,the creatures that were living in peace,all were in danger.The plans thrown by the fishermen destroyed the ecosystem,and if they did not do something soon,the reef Natal would have been lost forever.
-We need to act now! said Blue resolutely.Around him,the reef dolphins,his childhood friends,listened to him.For her,he was also a coral,an energetic and fast dolphin,and Finn,a playful dolphin,who knew all the secrets of the ocean.
-But how will we stop them? There are too many! Finn said worriedly.
-We don't have to face them directly,Blue replied.We just show them that the ocean is stronger than them.First,Blue and his friends were hiding among the corals and noticed the activity of fishermen.Their nets covered large areas of the reef.The people threw bait to attract the fish,

and some smaller creatures were caught without escape.
-We must move quickly,Coral said.If there are still a few days,nothing will remain in the reef!
-Then let's work together,Blue said.We must break their plans and make them leave.Blue proposed a three steps plan:

Distracting - a group of dolphins would create waves and attract the attention of fishermen away from the reef.
The release of nets - other dolphins and marine creatures were to cut the nets and release the captive fish.
Creating a powerful current-using ocean currents,dolphins could push the boats offshore,away from the reef.
They all agree.The Ocean would fight back.
Coral and a group of dolphins swim to the fishermen's boats and began to jump out of the water,making acrobatic movements.
-Hey! Look! Dolphin! cried one of the fishermen.The people took the rooms and forgot for a few fishing moments.It was a spectacular view,and the fishermen seemed a magical moment.Finn and a few larger fish began to pull the heavy nets,trying to undo their knots.

The reef octopus used their tentacles to weaken the ties,while Blue was pushing the nets,creating holes where the fish could escape.
-Faster! We don't have much time! Finn said.Blue moves quickly and used a sharp stone on the bottom of the ocean to cut the last threads that held the nets.Sometimes,one of the fishermen noticed what was happening.
-Places! They break! People tried to pick them up,but it was too late.You've escaped! Blue knew that fishermen did not like to fish in agitated waters.If they,the dolphins,could create a strong current,the boats would have removed alone.He and the other dolphins swim in rapid circles,creating an underwater whirl.He moves,pushing boats and raising growing waves.
-What happens?! shouted one of the fishermen,trying to control the boat.The values rose,and the boats were chaotic.The peasants tried to raise their nets and start the engines,but the current was too strong.One,they were moving away from the reef.Departed in the distance,the dolphins slowed down and looked around.
-I succeed! Coral screamed,jumping from the water.
-The ocean helped us, because we helped him too,Blue said, looking at the reef that was still shining under the sun.Finn approached and touched Blue's muzzle.
-You became a true ocean protector,Blue.Delfinii,Fish,Catrackers,even the smallest creatures in the reef,gathered around them, happy.Their home was saved.But Blue knew this was the first battle.He always needed protection.And he was ready to fight for him anytime

Chapter 20: Final confrontation

The reef was still in danger.Although Blue and his friends managed to drive fishermen for a while,the boats were returning,this time more and more determined.People did not want to give up so easily.

-He is approaching again,and this time there are more,Coral said,looking worried.

-We can not let the reef fall prey to these invaders,Finn said.We must find a better solution.Blue knew they could not face them. People were strong,but the ocean had an advantage:the intelligence of his creatures.

-We will not fight directly with them,but we will scare them! We will use the ocean against them.Blue proposed a plan based on fear and unknown.People were afraid of what they did not understand.If the dolphins and other creatures of the ocean would have created strange illusions and phenomena,the fishermen could have believed that the reef was cursed or dangerous.

The plan had three parts:

The creation of an underwater fog-the-light fish and the octopus were to create a cloud of ink and phosphorescence around the boats, so that the fishermen no longer see what is happening.

The generation of mysterious sounds-the nearby dolphins and whales were to issue unusual sounds to scare people.

The simulation of a "huge creature" - by teamwork,dolphins were to create the illusion that a huge being lived in the reef,removing the definitive fishermen.The first phase: the ocean's fogs When the boats approached,a group of octopus,led by their friend,Octa,began to release thick ink clouds.Black and bright at the same time, as if an ocean vortex was preparing to swallow them.

-What is that?! cries one of the fishermen.

-I haven't seen something like that before! We have to get out of here!
-It is not stupid,it's just a natural reaction! said the captain.But ... I have to admit,it's weird ...
Second phase:voices from the depths

Then,out of the dark,strange sounds began to resonate.Delphins issued sound waves at an unusual pace,and the nearby whales responded with deep and vibrant moans.The peasants looked at each other,scared.
-How heard that?
-Sun ... as if something huge follows us! A wave of restlessness crossed the crews.People were brave,but the ocean was vast and full of mysteries.
Third phase:Colossal shadow
Now came the last part of the plan.Delphins swim in formation,moving in circles tightened underwater,lifting sand and shiny particles in the coral.Together,in the diffuse light of the-light fish,their silhouettes seemed to form a huge monster,with tentacles and a massive body rising from the depths.
-It's a monster! one of the fishermen screamed.

-It can not be true! said another,but gathered his equipment,preparing for the departure.
-I is clear that this place is not sure.The engines began to scream,and the boats turned off.A few minutes,the reef was free again.The depths broke out in cries of joy,jumping from the water in a sign of victory.Their reprint was saved,this time.In the area,knowing that the ocean will always be in danger,but that there will always be someone ready to defend it.

Chapter 21: The reef is reborn

After the fishermen left,the ocean was filled with a deep silence.The reef,so close to destruction,could finally breathe again.Covered by residues of rusty nets and hooks.The people who had hidden during the confrontation began to get out of their shelters,but the fear still persisted.
-We must rebuild the reef,Blue said,looking at his friends.We can't leave things that way.
-We need the help of everyone,Coral replied.If we unite,the ocean will recover! Blue knew he couldn't do this alone.The ocean was vast,but each creature had an essential role.Thus,every inhabitant of the reef received a task:
The octopuses began to remove the remains left behind by the fishermen,using their tentacles to gather the nets and hooks.
Dolphins worked together to transport healthy coral fragments and repositioned them in places where the reef had been destroyed.
Crusataces cleaned the sand on the bottom of the ocean,burying the metal debris and helping to naturally regenerate the ecosystem.

To spread the beneficial algae, accelerating the healing process of the corals. The man was not easy. The whole days, each life of the reef contributed to the restoration of their home. And the colorful fish had returned to swim among the delicate branches. One morning, Blue observed something that filled him with hope: a pair of sea guards dancing in gentle currents, something that had not happened long ago.
-This means that the reef begins to recover, Finn said, full of enthusiasm.
-Yes, but we have to remain vigilant, Coral added. We must take care of the ocean every day. In a short time, every creature that lived there again. They waved their tentacles, and the dolphins jumped to play through the waves. But above all, a lesson had been learned. Balue and his friends understood that the ocean needed constant protection. They were no longer just the inhabitants of the reef, now they were his guards.
-Anything would happen, we will always be here to defend the ocean, Blue said, looking at the infinite blue. And so, the reef was reborn, and with him, the hope of a better future.

Chapter 22: A new adventure

After the reef recovered, Blue believed that he could enjoy peace. But the ocean had other plans for him. One night, while swimming under the light of the moon, the old Arlo called him aside.

-Blue, you did something extraordinary by saving the reef. But your duty has not ended yet, said the turtle in a serious voice. Blue looked at him curiously.

-What is it about, Arlo? The old turtle sighed deep and continues:

-the magic artifact you have protected cannot stay here. His power is too big and too dangerous if he reaches the wrong hands. You must take him to the ocean sanctuary, a sacred place where he will be protected. Gold chill. Another trip? He had just turned, and now he had to leave again?

-Where is this sanctuary?

-Beyond the land of ice, in a place where only those with a clean heart can reach. He understood that he had no choice.

-Gine, Arlo. I will take care of this. The next day, Blue told his friends about the mission he had received.

-Before the land of ice? Coral exclaims. There are cold and dangerous waters!

-And unknown creatures, Finn added, worried.

-I know, but I have to do this. The ocean is up to me. Coral and Finn nodded, understanding that Blue could not be stopped. So they helped him to prepare.

-He needed supplies, Coral said, bringing algae rich in energy.

-And the guide, Finn added. The arlo can show you a map of safe currents.

-Thank you, friends. I do not know what I would do without you. At dawn, Blue started on the journey. The water became colder as it was approaching the glacies. The lively reef. The water became colder,

and the currents changed. He felt like the salty air stuck his smooth skin, but the thought he had pushed him forward. About the creatures that lived there were not soothing.
-Are they really monsters in those waters? Blue asked, reminding Arlo's warnings. But he had no time for fears. He had to take the artifact to the oceanic sanctuary. As far as he went to the north, the waves became harsher. The current had changed, pulling him in unexpected directions.
-I must stay concentrated, Blue thought, struggling to maintain his direction. Then, suddenly, he felt a shadow passing by him. Something big was moving through the water, following him. He slowed his pace, trying to distinguish what it was. Then, behind a glacier, a huge figure appeared. It was a shark-white, one of the greatest predators of the ocean.
-What do we have here? He mumbled the shark, with his cold eyes, fixing Blue. The Delfin swallowed in the century. He could not fight with such a monster.
-Welcome! I am not looking for problems. I just try to get to the oceanic sanctuary.
-Sanctuar? No one passes here without my permission! Blue knew

he had to find a way to escape.But how could he avoid such a big shark? Before the shark approached too much,a loud sound sounded through the water.A huge whale came out of the dark, swimming between Blue and Shark.
-Limen him alone, Zephyr,said the whale in a deep and imposing voice.
-Good luck,dolphinule.But be careful where you go! Then the shark disappeared in the dark.Balue breathed in relief.He had returned to a step again.
-Thank you! he told the whale.How do you call yourself?
-Nalu.I heard of you,Blue.You are the dolphin that saved the reef.
-You know me? Blue asked surprised.
-The ocean tells its stories,Nalu said,smiling.If you need help,I can guide you to the sanctuar.Blue felt a wave of hope.He was not alone on this adventure.With a new ally on his side,he was ready to continue his the journey.The oceanic sanctuary was waiting for him.

Chapter 23: Final attempts

With every moment, Blue felt that he was approaching the destination. The oceanic senior was no longer just a legend, but a real place, just a few miles away. But the road was not easy. In front of him stretched the most dangerous part of the journey, The sea of shadows. The poverty said that no one had ever passed through those waters without wandering. The guards were strong, the darkness ruled, and the predators were shaking.

-I have to be prepared, Blue thought, looking forward. While swimming further, you feel how the water around it begins to move differently. A huge whirl formed right in front of him!

-Oh, no! The whirlwind caught him in the middle of him, pulling him down. Blue tried to swim against the current, but it was too strong.

-If I fight, I just lose my energy! Blue thought. He had to find another solution. Instead of being resistant, he was wearing a power point, looking for an output. His eyes ran through the water, analyzing the flow of the movement. Then, he noticed a space where the current was weaker.

-This is my chance! With all the strength, Blue used his tail to propel himself in that direction. He breathed deeply. He had taken on the first obstacle. As far as he went, the light began to disappear. Nor could the dangers be avoided. Suddenly, you heard a strange sound. A weak but threatening strip. Then, out of the dark, something appeared. A bench of electric angles!

-It's not good, it's not good at all! Blue thought, giving back. The angles began to approach, moving like shadows. If they touched it, they could paralyze it. Blue knew he couldn't face them, but he remembered a trick he had learned from Arlo.

-When you are in the dark, listen to the water.

He closed his eyes and stopped moving.He focused all his senses on the water vibrations.Then you felt something,a small current that came from another direction.

-There I have to go! Without opening his eyes,Blue swims quickly to that current.He was just a few centimeters of anhils,but they had not touched him.When he opened his eyes again,it was safe.The dark water was behind.He had one last obstacle.In the distance, large silhouettes were moving through the water.They were shark! He couldn't avoid them,they had already noticed it.

-I will not give up now! He looked around quickly, looking for a place to hide.Then he saw a reef of spinos.

-If I can slip among them,the sharks will not be able to follow me! He swam as fast as he could, approaching the reef.The roots were in his footsteps,but Blue was more agile.He was among the rocks,slipping among the narrow spaces.The rest tried to follow him,but their rigid swimming did not allow them to slip.

-Ready! I'm safe! After the predators moved away,Blue continued his way.He was close to the sanctuar.With each swim,Blue felt that he was getting closer to his destination.The oceanic sect,the place where he had to carry the magic artifact.He was testing the decision.Despite the fatigue,he kept his pace.He had been riding,he had escaped the dark waters and he had trimmed the sharks.But he could not let the guard down.Any moment of inattention could be fatal.To hope that the biggest obstacles had passed.But, suddenly,he felt a change.A strange cold encompassed him.

-What happens? he whispered.From the fog,a huge silhouette appeared.It was a gigantic jellyfish,with light tentacles and a strange aura.

-Who are you? he asked,trying to keep his calm.The bride seemed to study it.Then,a gentle, but powerful voice,echoed in his mind.

-Are you the one who wears the artifact? Blue was fluttering.He hadn't talked to him in this way.

-Yes. I have to take him to the oceanic sanctuary Jellyfish wave his tentacles and create a circle of light around Blue.

-The last attempt is here.In order to step into the sanctuary,you have to prove your clean heart.

-How can i do that?

-No powerful,not at speed.And in truth.The Jellyfish let his tentacles

float around Blue,and a wave of memories overwhelmed him.His struggles with the dangers of the ocean.Then you feel a deep question in his mind.
-Why do you do this,Blue? Blue inspires deep.Why? He could have said that he was out of curiosity.Or from the desire for adventure. But the truth was another.
-because the ocean needs protection.Because I want my family and friends to be safe.
-Then,you passed the test.The fog nier was scattered,and in front of Blue something incredible appeared.It was a place as Blue had never seen.In the center,on a pedestal covered by algae,was the place where the artifact had to place slowly swimming,feeling that each movement was important.Arrived in front of the pedestal,removed the artifact from the neck and carefully placed it.A wave of energy spread through the water.The ocean was protected again.And Blue,the curious dolphin who had started in a simple adventure,had become a real hero.

Chapter 24: Sacrifice

Blue looked at the artifact shining on the pedestal,feeling in the depths that something was going to change forever.The ocean shook around him,as if the whole underwater world was waiting for what was going to happen.Suddenly,a wave of energy encompassed him.And a deep voice echoed in his mind:
-You do not end,Blue.In order for the artifact to fulfill its purpose,you must pay a price.
The dolphin felt a cold chill on the back.He had never thought he would have to give up something.
-What do I have to do? A gentle light enveloped him,and in front

of him appeared a vision.He saw his native reef,family,friends.Then the voice came back.

-For the artifact to protect the ocean,you have to give up what you love the most.

-It I give up? But...the ocean is my life.My family.He could not refuse.He had to make a decision.By thinking about everything he had gone through,Blue realized what the sacrifice meant.It was not about suffering,but doing what was correct,regardless of the price.He had to leave the reef forever.He wanted to return home,to enjoy the hot waters,his friends.But if the ocean needed him elsewhere? What if his destiny was to be a protector?

Blue felt a pain in my soul.But I know this was the right choice.

-Accept.a wave of light spread around,and the artifact was completely activated.The ocean seemed to vibrate with it.To him,as if the whole world was waiting for his decision.The artifact,a brilliant pearl called the pearl of time surrounded by ancient symbols,slightly pulled with a blue light.

-Any power requires a balance.If the artifact has to protect the ocean,you have to leave something behind.Blue feels his heart beats

faster.Part of him wanted to refuse,but he knew that the ocean,his family,friends,all creatures which he had met,they depended on his choice.
-What do I have to give up? he asked,hoping that the sacrifice would not be too painful.As far as his question was floating in the water,a wave of memories hit him.He saw his parents,the reef,the laughter of his friends,play with the other dolphins,the warm rays of the sun who penetrated through water.All these things were so dear to him ...
-You have to choose,Blue.The ocean offers you a lot,but to protect everything you love,you have to leave some of you behind.Delfin feels how emotions are enveloped in his soul.He begins to breathe deeply,to clear his thoughts.What part of him would be willing to lose for the good of others? Then,the understanding hit him like a strong wave:he had to give up his house.He was hard to accept this thought,but he realized that if he really wanted to protect the ocean,he could not only stay in his native reef.He leaves and becomes a protector of the waters of the whole world.Its friend was heading for Artifact,and the voice from the depths was again heard:
-You understand the sacrifice.Do you accept your destiny? Blue closed his eyes for a moment,remembering each lesson he had learned on his journey.Each danger,every friend he had made,every obstacle that had turned him into a stronger dolphin.With a last look Towards the vast ocean,he looked up at Artifact and whispered:
-Yes.I accept my destiny.At that moment,the artifact lights up suddenly,and a wave of energy spread through the water,hugging the whole ocean in a protective glow.At home,to live in the safety of the reef,to be again only a young and worry free dolphin.Instead,you feel something new filled it:a greater purpose,a call to the unknown.

As the light fades,Blue realized that the ocean was waiting for him.He did not belong to one place.Now,the whole sea was his house.

Chapter 25: Meeting

Blue advanced through the clear waters,approaching his native reef.The heart was beating them quickly,so many things had changed since he had left.Did the reef look the same? As he approached,he felt a wave of emotion.The reef was more alive than ever! The corals sparkled in vibrant colors,fish banks danced at the rate of currents,and the dolphins in his colony were worried.It was as if the whole ocean celebrated his return.Then,a known sound pierced his hearing, it was his mother's call.
-Blue! From nowhere,the dolphins turned to him,surrounding him with joy.His mother,his eyes sparkling with emotion,hugged him in the way of dolphins, rubbing his muzzle of his.
-You back!
-I turned,Blue said, feeling a knot in his throat.Then,the whole colony burst into cheers and holiday songs.Old and we surrounded him,asking him about his journey.Somehow there,lifting his head with a wise smile.
-I always knew you would succeed,chickens.Blue smiled.He felt a deep silence,as if the ocean thanked them for everything he had done.Then one of the dolphins shouted:
-Let's celebrate Blue! He protected the ocean and saved the reef! The whole colony burst into a dance of the waters.Delphins jumped through the waves, making pirouettes,while the colorful fish joined them,creating an underwater show and colors.He felt completely.Blue was left by the warm waves, surrounded by his friends and family.It was a moment that he had imagined countless times along the way of his adventure,but the reality was even more beautiful than the dream.

While dolphins From the colony they expressed their joy through spectacular jumps,Blue felt the warmth of the reef hugging it again.The collars sparkled under the filtered light of the sun,the anemones were slightly swinging,and the fish banks changed their direction as vivid colors. Blue's mother did not He could still detach from him.He was gently touching the muzzle,checking him as if he couldn't believe that her son had really turned.

-You raised, Blue.Her eyes were full of emotion.

-I learned a lot,he said, looking at the vast ocean who had called him in the unknown.

-Well,you came back,little girl.I was going to succeed,but I have to admit,I didn't expect to come back so quickly.Balue chuckles.

-Sometimes I did not expect to succeed.Taking,everyone in the reef gathered around Blue,eager to listen to the stories about his trip.

-Tell us, Blue! How did you find the artifact?

-Have you seen huge creatures?

-How did you get rid of the dark caves? Blue took a moment to gather his thoughts.He remembered the powerful currents who removed him from the initial route,the unexpected meeting with Arlo,the mystery of the deep fish and the creatures he had known on the road. He remembered the dangers Facing, but also by the friendly friendships. Then, they began to tell. Delphins were listening as Blue spoke to them about the lost city of the corals, about the pearl thieves and the huge creature in the depths, which was not a monster, but Only alone. When he reached the part where he had to give up a important thing for him to save the ocean, his voice softens.

-But it was not in vain. The artifact is now safe, and the ocean is protected. A silence full of respect is on the reef. They all understood Blue's sacrifice. They were not just coming back as a dolphin who went on an adventure, but as a true ocean protector. After the story was over, the reef dolphins began to spin in large circles, in a large circles.

-A old dance of their ancestors, as a sign of gratitude. The whole reef vibration of life, celebrating Blue, the hero who had returned home.

-To you never forget, Blue. The adequate courage does not just mean to face dangers, but to have an open heart to learn and protect what you love. To the vast ocean. His adventures were not over. But for the first time, he felt exactly where he had to be.

Chapter 26: Lessons learned

After days of holidays and joy,Blue withdrew to have a moment of silence.He was carried by the gentle currents of the reef and sat on a soft sand bed, looking at the sky above the water.Everything seemed the same as before,but he felt that he was no longer the same dolphin who had gone on that adventure.In his mind the images of the journey took place.He remembered the enthusiasm from the beginning,the emotion of the unknown,the obstacles that put him to the test and the moments when a I felt he would not succeed.But most,he remembered those he met on the road.He thought of Arlo,the wise turtle,who had offered him essential advice on the ocean and the wisdom of those who lived more.Blue would have been lost in the unknown.
Then he remembered the-light fish that helped him to find the exit from the dark fish.Even the youngest of the creatures of the ocean could be unexpected rescuers.They thought of the huge creature in the abyss,who was not a monster,but only alone.In Blue's world, sometimes fear came only from misunderstanding.And then,the tape band thieves.Not all the inhabitants of the ocean were friendly,but every meeting taught him something.Blue realizes that no adventure can be lived alone.Even The biggest challenges could be overcome with the help of friends and those who believed in you.Thinking about all the times when he was about to give up.The powerful currents who removed him from the route,the storm that threw him to the unknown island,the confrontation with the shark,the meeting with the thieves.But every time,instead of being defeated by fear,he gathered his powers and continued.They courage does not mean not to feel fear,but to find your power to move on in spite of it.Blue has now understood that every challenge was a test,

every obstacle,a lesson.Then he remembered the moment when a He had to give up something important for him to complete the mission.The scripic had been hard,but necessary.Sometimes,to protect what you love,you have to leave something behind.Once the artifact was placed in its place,the ocean and- he regained balance.And although Blue no longer had that precious object,he had won something more valuable,knowledge,wisdom and a stronger heart.Blue felt like a wave of tranquility includes him.Now he understood that the adventure was not just about Artifact,treasures or dangers,but about what he learned about himself and the ocean.He was no longer just a curious young dolphin.Now he was a protector of the ocean,a stories bearer,a symbol of courage.He looked up and looked The lively reef.This was his house,the place he loved and was ready to protect him.While he was floating quietly among the corals,Blue observed how the sun's rays penetrated through the water,playing the fish scales and coloring The reef in magical shades.Everything seemed more beautiful than before,as if the ocean itself recognized his effort and thanked them for what he had done.But although everything seemed in his place, something in Blue had changed.Curious dolphin,but a dolphin who understood the true meaning of adventure and responsibility.Blue remembered the words of old Arlo, the wise turtle that had been a guide at the beginning of the journey:

-True power does not come from speed or strength,but from knowledge and ability to learn from every experience.When he had left the reef,he thought he had to be brave and venture into the unknown.Now he understood that the real courage is not Just the boldness to explore,but also the wisdom to learn from mistakes,to listen to the advice of the wisest and to take care of others.Without the help of his friends,without the teachings he received along the way,no He would never have managed to protect the ocean.Blue looked at his group of friends,dolphins who had accompanied him on his return.They were all there:

Lina,the dolphin that always encouraged him to go further.

Arlo,who,although old,had swam with him a part of the road and had always offered precious advice.

The group of fish-light,which had guided him through the darkness of the fish.

The colony of dolphins on the secret island,who told him about Artifact and offered him an important mission.

Each of them played a role in his story,and Blue felt that the adventure was not only his, but of all those who helped him.

-A hero is never alone.Putting comes from those who believe in you and Of the ones you love.While swimming with his friends, Blue knew that the ocean would always need protectors.If there was a magic artifact,there may be other secrets under waves.If there were dangers that had threatened the reef, There will be others.But this time,Blue was no longer afraid.Was prepared.

-Each end is actually a new beginning.

Chapter 27: A new beginning

Blue was floating quietly above the reef, looking at the life of normal. The people were swimming, the corals had regained their vibrant colors, and the sun's rays were played in the gentle waves. With his mission. Now he had a new purpose, to become a protector of the ocean and to teach others the importance of nature and harmony between the living. One morning, a group of young dolphins followed him with admiration, curious to find out more About his adventures. Blue smiled and began to tell them about the dangers he had gone through, but also about the friends he had won along the way.

-The courage does not mean only to face the dangers, but also to take care of those around you, Blue said. And to become reef protectors. Travel again, but this time not to look for treasures or magical artifacts, but to carry a message of unity and responsibility to all the creatures of the ocean. They were going, they said the story of the

reef,they warned about the dangers of people and they learned other species on how to how to protect nature.
- If we work together,nothing can destroy our house,Blue told each new group he met.Had inspired others to protect the ocean in their turn.The-light-lumine used their glow to guide the lost life.The old-old old people told young people about the importance of natural balance.Delfini patrolled reefs and made sure that everything was in harmony.Of a single hero.Blue floated above the reef,feeling the slight expression of the marine currents that enveloped him as a warm hug.Everything seemed more alive than ever,colored fish banks danced among the corals,and the rays of the sun penetrated among the waters, hugging the world with an underwater world.Golden light.After so many adventures,he felt changed.It was not just a curious dolphin who dreamed of remote places.Now he was a protector of the ocean.Every day,he met with groups of young dolphins,who were looking at him with big,curious eyes,wanting to find out about his travels.
-The ocean is our house,but also a place full of mysteries,said Blue.We must explore it with respect and protect it from dangers.The dolphins were listening to him.They wanted to know how he had faced the storm,how he escaped from shark and how he had managed to protect the magic artifact.But Blue always explained that the biggest lesson he had learned was that a true hero was not alone.
- Friendship and wisdom are the greatest powers we have,he said.But to spread a message of unity and protection of the ocean.They met with fish banks, turtles and even some of the creatures that Blue had encountered on his journey.Each species played in the ocean,And if they worked together,they could maintain the fragile balance of nature.

- If we unite our forces,we can make the ocean a safer place for all,said Blue anywhere.Even some sharks,who had been considered dangerous before, understood that they had a role in the trophic chain of the ocean.And Blue's story spread throughout the ocean.Not because he had been a hero who had saved the reef,but because he had inspired a whole generation of nature protectors.The old-old old people told the young people about his courage and kindness.Everything was in harmony.Peace-Lumina continued to guide traveled travelers through dark waters.And Blue? He knew that the ocean did not need a single hero,but a whole community to protect him.Like his coral friend,Blue formed a beautiful family,and after Blue's disappearance,his descendants continued his work.

Chapter 28: Blue's legend

Time passed,and the ocean continued to breathe in its mysterious rhythm,carrying the echoes of the past through its endless waves.Blue was no longer a name,it was a legend.His trips,about the courage with which he protected the reef and about the wisdom he shared with all.In the quiet nights,when the moon casts the silver light over the waters,the young dolphins gathered around the elders and listened with their souls:
- There was once a Dolphin named Blue,who dared to explore the unknown,who defeated dangers and united the ocean.Blue's legend was not just about adventures and treasures.It was about the courage to face fear,about the power of friendship and about Respect for the ocean.In every corner of the sea, the dolphins began to live according to its principles:to help each other,to respect nature and to fight for the balance of the waters.It was said that,in the serene nights,if you listened

carefully, You could hear the sound of a dolphin that jumped among the waves, carried by the wind. They thought it was just a myth. But others knew the truth: Blue had not just been a hero of the past. He lived in every wave, in every dolphin who carried further inheritance. And so, Blue's story would never be forgotten. The time had passed, but Blue's name had not been lost in the depths of forgetting. The ocean. In each generation, new dolphin chicks were growing with the desire to follow the example. Some dreamed to explore the unknown depths, others wanted to protect the reef, and others hoped to become as wise and brave as Blue. A group of young dolphins gathered near the rock of the Moon, the place where the elders shared their stories. A albino dolphin, with sparkling eyes, approached with emotion:

-Tell us again about Blue! About how the ocean saved! An old dolphin, with the skin marked by years and wisdom, smiled and began to speak:

-Blue was not an ordinary dolphin. He had the courage to face the unknown and change our world forever. He brought peace, saved the reef and showed that true power does not come from force, but from the heart. They looked at each other with enthusiasm.

-Do you think Blue is there,somewhere? asked a dolphin chicken,with big and curious eyes.The old man laughed slowly.
-Maybe Blue no longer swims among us,but he lives in every wave,in every breeze,in every dolphin who follows his dream without fear.If you ever feel lost, look at the stars reflected in the water.Blue is there,watching over the ocean.In the blue depths,Blue's reef was glowing more beautifully.Wisdom. Over now,Blue had left a strong inheritance:a world in which the ocean was not only a place of survival,but a home,protected and respected by all its inhabitants.His legend was not just a story,it was a lesson.And as long as the waves continued to dance under the moon,and the dolphins swam free through the sea,Blue's name would live forever.

Epilogue:

The ocean continued to breathe in its eternal rhythm,the waves caressing the reefs,and the currents wearing stories from one corner of the sea to another. Time had passed, but Blue's adventure remained alive in the hearts of those who had known him.He was home,Blue was no longer the same young dolphin who had left with his heart.The inhabitants of the reef looked at him with admiration,and the young dolphins gathered around him,asking them to tell them about the amazing creatures he had encountered,about the frightening storms and about the unforgettable friends he had made along his journey.But Blue knew that his story had not ended here.The ocean was vast,full of mysteries waiting to be discovered.Blue looked beyond the horizon. The shock that other adventures would come,that the ocean will again ask for the courage and the desire to explore.And,although he had found his place in the reef,his soul belonged to the whole ocean.His pink became a legend,but the legend was not the end.It was just the beginning of something new.With one last look at the loved ones,Blue started again,swimming to the endless horizon.

Copyright

(C)

Bucur Loredan 10-02-2025
Birmingham U.K.